Japanese warplanes swarm U.S. ships and airfields at Pearl Harbor during the first wave of the surprise attack on December 7, 1941. Later a tattered Old Glory (opposite) from the sunken battleship *California* is pulled from the water.

Front cover: Sailors at Ford Island Naval Air Station watch a massive explosion aboard the destroyer *Shaw* across the channel.

More than a million pounds of gunpowder explodes inside the *Arizona* during the first minutes of the attack on Battleship Row, collapsing the foremast (opposite) and killing about a thousand American sailors, including 24 sets of brothers and a father and son.

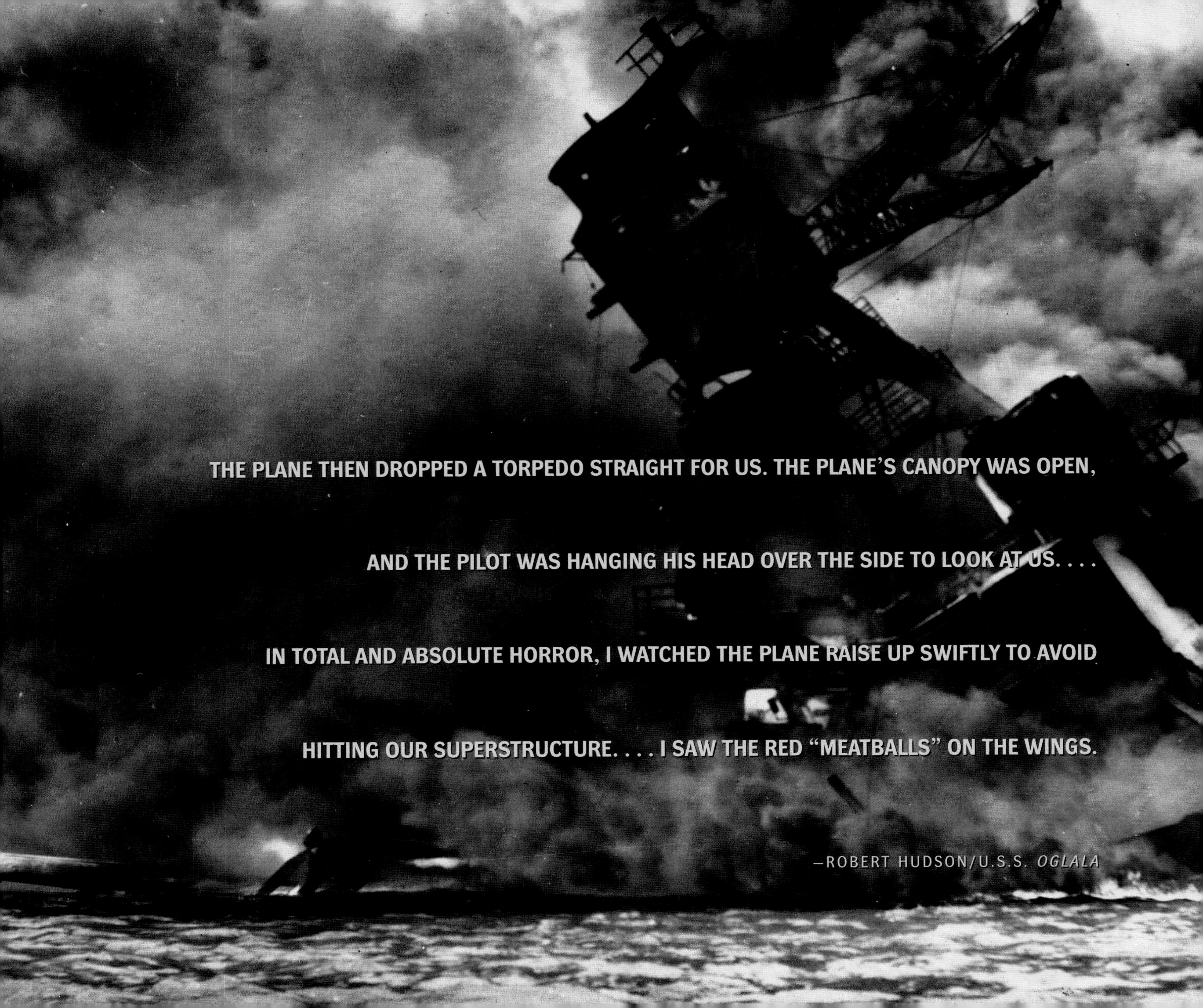

THE PLANE THEN DROPPED A TORPEDO STRAIGHT FOR US. THE PLANE'S CANOPY WAS OPEN,

AND THE PILOT WAS HANGING HIS HEAD OVER THE SIDE TO LOOK AT US. . . .

IN TOTAL AND ABSOLUTE HORROR, I WATCHED THE PLANE RAISE UP SWIFTLY TO AVOID

HITTING OUR SUPERSTRUCTURE. . . . I SAW THE RED "MEATBALLS" ON THE WINGS.

—ROBERT HUDSON/U.S.S. *OGLALA*

**In the lazy days before the war, sunbathers relaxing on the sand at Honolulu's Waikiki Beach enjoy a dramatic view of Diamond Head.**

## The Approach of War

BY **PETER MILLER** THE DAY BEFORE THAT AWFUL SUNDAY MORNING IN 1941 NO ONE IN HONOLULU EXPECTED TO BE ATTACKED. NOT THE BEARCATS OF WILLAMETTE COLLEGE, WHO'D FLOWN IN FROM OREGON TO PLAY THE FOOTBALL TEAM FROM THE UNIVERSITY OF HAWAII. NOT THE MUSICIANS FROM THE U.S.S. *PENNSYLVANIA*, WHO BATTLED THREE OTHER GROUPS FOR BRAGGING RIGHTS AS THE BEST BAND IN THE FLEET. NOT THE ARMY'S COMMANDING GENERAL, WHO ATTENDED THE ANNUAL CHARITY SHOW AT THE OFFICERS' CLUB. NOT THE COMMANDER OF THE NAVY'S PACIFIC FLEET, WHO WENT TO BED EARLY TO PREPARE FOR A ROUND OF GOLF THE NEXT MORNING. BUT THEY SHOULD HAVE EXPECTED IT. THE SIGNS WERE EVERYWHERE. RELATIONS BETWEEN JAPAN AND THE UNITED STATES HAD BEEN TEETERING ON THE BRINK OF HOSTILITIES FOR MONTHS. THE U.S. AMBASSADOR TO JAPAN HAD CABLED WASHINGTON WITH WARNINGS OF IMMINENT WAR. CODED MESSAGES BETWEEN TOKYO AND SPIES IN HAWAII HAD BEEN INTERCEPTED. SIX JAPANESE AIRCRAFT CARRIERS HAD DISAPPEARED AND WERE ASSUMED TO BE ON THE MOVE.

Looking back after six decades, it's difficult to imagine how so many clues were missed or ignored—as difficult as it is to understand why Japan attacked in the first place.

The causes of the war were complex. But one direct road to Pearl Harbor began on a bridge outside Beijing, where Chinese soldiers skirmished with a Japanese patrol on July 7, 1937. Six years earlier Japanese Army officers had seized control of China's northern province of Manchuria. In 1937 Japan used the "China incident" as an excuse to push south, attacking major cities along the coast. During the "rape of Nanking," the Chinese capital at the time, Japanese troops massacred at least 40,000 civilians, shocking the American public but not crushing Chinese resistance. A costly guerrilla war dragged on for years.

The conflict drove a solid wedge between Japan and the United States. At first President Franklin D. Roosevelt condemned Japan's invasion of China, declaring a "moral embargo" against trade of military goods with Japan. Then when Japanese troops landed in French Indochina in 1941, he froze Japanese assets in the United States and cut off Japan's critical supplies of oil from the U.S. To Japanese leaders his actions threatened the very survival of their nation, which they believed depended upon further expansion into Southeast Asia. Forming an alliance with Germany and Italy, the Japanese military set its sights on British Malaya, the Dutch East Indies, and the Philippines, a U.S. commonwealth. Without abundant new supplies of tin, rubber, oil, and other resources, Japan feared it could not fulfill its destiny to rule Asia.

War now appeared inevitable between Japan and the United States. For years the U.S. ambassador to Tokyo, Joseph C. Grew, had warned of the "swashbuckling temper" of the Japanese military. Hitler's bold conquests in Europe, he said, had "gone to the Japanese head like strong wine." Yet the daring plan to bomb Pearl Harbor came not from a young warrior itching to fight, but rather from a 57-year-old veteran deeply opposed to war with America. Adm. Isoroku Yamamoto, commander in chief of Japan's Combined Fleet, had studied at Harvard University and served as a naval attaché in Washington. Having witnessed America's industrial strength and vast resources, he doubted Japan's chances for ultimate victory. "If I am told to fight regardless of the consequences," he told Japan's premier, "I shall run wild for the first six months or a year, but I have utterly no confidence for the second or third year." So unpopular had Yamamoto become to Japan's military extremists that a bounty was said to have been offered for his assassination.

Once Yamamoto was convinced that war was unavoidable, however, he reached a startling conclusion: Instead of waiting for the U.S. to venture close to Japanese waters, where Japan's navy could fight a defensive slug out, Japan should launch a surprise

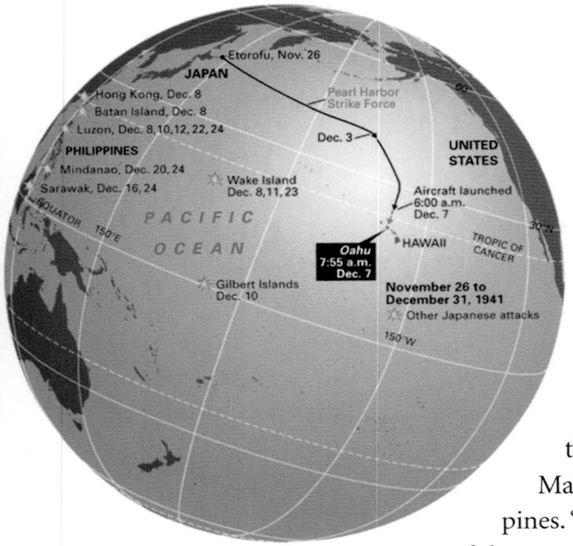

To avoid detection, the Japanese fleet of six aircraft carriers and 26 escorts takes a northern route across the Pacific on its 12-day, 4,000-mile voyage to Hawaii, avoiding commercial sea-lanes. The carefree island life symbolized by girls posing with surfboards (opposite) on Waikiki Beach will soon come to an end.

attack on Pearl Harbor to deliver an early knockout punch. If Japan could destroy the U.S. Pacific Fleet in one preemptive strike, it could set up an impenetrable line of defense across the Pacific before America could build more ships. By then it would be too late for the U.S. to challenge Japan's conquest of Malaya, the Dutch East Indies, and the Philippines. "We should do our very best at the outset of the war with the United States," he wrote a navy colleague, ". . . to decide the fate of the war on the very first day."

Even as the Japanese prepared for war, however, American leaders seemed blind to the approaching danger, suffering from what one Pearl Harbor veteran described as the "supreme overconfidence" of a great athlete. The idea of Japan's attacking the powerful U.S. Pacific Fleet in Hawaii, in particular, was unthinkable. "The Island of Oahu, due to its fortifications, its garrison, and its physical characteristics, is believed to be the strongest fortress in the world," said Gen. George C. Marshall, the U.S. Army Chief of Staff. Speaking on the day before the attack, Senator Owen Brewster of Maine boasted that the U.S. Navy "can defeat the Japanese Navy, any place and at any time." Even President Roosevelt and his top advisers, who were reading Tokyo's secret diplomatic messages, failed to recognize the imminent danger to Hawaii.

The two officers most responsible for defending Pearl Harbor were caught equally unprepared for the assault. The commander in chief of the U.S. Pacific Fleet, Adm. Husband E. Kimmel, was convinced that Japan would strike in Southeast Asia, not Hawaii. Even after an urgent "war warning" to Pacific bases from Washington on November 27, stating that "an aggressive move by Japan is expected within the next few days," Kimmel took no special precautions at Pearl Harbor. No ships were sent to sea, no long-range patrols ordered for Navy scout planes. The commander of the Army's Hawaiian Department, Lt. Gen. Walter C. Short, was more worried about sabotage by Hawaii's 160,000 residents of Japanese ancestry than about a surprise attack by Tokyo. When he read the "war warning" message on November 27, he ordered a "Number 1 Alert," calling for "a defense against sabotage, espionage, and subversive activities without any threat from the outside." Instead of taking measures to ensure that his warplanes could respond swiftly to an attack, he ordered ammunition to be locked up in boxes to prevent theft by locals and his aircraft parked in tight groups out in the open, where they could be easily protected from saboteurs. As a result, they were neatly lined up like sitting ducks when the Japanese bombers swooped in.

To be fair, Hawaii's military leaders might have defended Pearl Harbor better if America's intelligence agencies had been more alert and had passed along crucial information sooner. Only a few weeks after Admiral Yamamoto began discussing Operation Hawaii with other Japanese naval officers, Ambassador Grew picked up an alarming rumor in Tokyo. Grew cabled Washington that a respected Peruvian diplomat had told a member of Grew's staff that "he had heard from many sources including a Japanese source that the Japanese military forces planned, in the event of trouble with the United States, to attempt a surprise mass attack on Pearl Harbor using all of their military facilities." This report was circulated at the State Department and Navy Department, where it landed on the desk of Comdr. Arthur H. McCollum, chief of the Far Eastern

Section of the Office of Naval Intelligence. An expert on Japan, having lived there for years before being assigned to Washington, McCollum dismissed the idea. "The Division of Naval Intelligence places no credence in these rumors," he wrote to Admiral Kimmel, summarizing Grew's report. "Furthermore, based on known data regarding the present disposition and employment of Japanese naval and army forces, no move against Pearl Harbor appears imminent or planned for in the foreseeable future." The rumor was forgotten.

Although the U.S. had broken the codes for Japanese diplomatic messages in the summer of 1940, Admiral Kimmel and General Short were not getting information they needed. Among the documents flooding cryptographers in Washington were cables from Takeo Yoshikawa, a spy in the Japanese consulate in Honolulu. In addition to his other duties Yoshikawa had regularly posed as a tourist in a bright aloha shirt, taking commercial sightseeing flights above Oahu, then reporting back to Tokyo on the number and types of warships in Pearl Harbor. As December 7 approached, his handlers in Tokyo stepped up their questions: How long did U.S. warships remain at anchor? On what day of the week would there be the most ships in the harbor? Do the battleships have torpedo nets? Were there any observation balloons over Pearl Harbor? Because Yoshikawa was never identified as a spy, his reports were ignored by intelligence experts in Washington. In his next-to-last cable, on December 6, he concluded, "I imagine that in all probability there is considerable opportunity left to take advantage for a surprise attack against these places." Intercepted by U.S. intelligence like the others from Yoshikawa, this cable was not given priority for decoding. It sat in a pile of unread messages until Monday afternoon, December 8.

Yet another chance to sound the alert came at 6:45 Sunday morning, when the destroyer *Ward* spotted and fired upon a midget submarine near the entrance to the Pearl Harbor channel. The vessel was one of 32 Japanese submarines then encircling Oahu. Their mission was to spy on the base, torpedo escaping ships, and protect the Japanese carriers, which had yet to launch their planes. The *Ward*'s captain reported its action to the district watch officer, radioing that "we have attacked, fired upon, and dropped depth charges upon submarine operating in defensive sea area." But the urgency of the message was lost as the duty officer relayed the report to a second watch officer, who was delayed by busy signals in telephoning a third officer, who called Admiral Kimmel at home. Having recently dealt with numerous false alarms relating to submarines in the area, Kimmel reacted skeptically, deciding to "wait for verification." By that time, the Japanese bombers were on their way.

Incredibly, the Japanese aircraft were spotted by two U.S. Army radar operators at 7:02 a.m., while the planes were still more than 130 miles away. Even that wasn't enough to rouse Pearl Harbor into action. Pvt. Joseph L. Lockard had been training Pvt. George Elliott on the Opana mobile radar unit above Kahuku Point on Oahu's northern coast when the pair saw an enormous blip on the screen, bigger than anything Lockard had ever seen before—probably "more than 50" planes. They were supposed to have turned the radar off at 7 a.m. at the end of their daily three-hour watch, following General Short's directives. However, the breakfast truck had been late, so they'd decided to keep the radar unit on. Elliott called the switchboard operator at the Fort Shafter information center, who passed the message along to the pursuit officer, Lt. Kermit Tyler. Returning the call, Tyler, a fighter pilot manning the desk temporarily, spoke with Lockard, who told him they were continuing to track what appeared to be "an unusually large flight" racing in from almost due north. Remembering that a flight of American B-17 bombers was due to arrive from the mainland that morning, Tyler told Lockard, "Well, don't worry about it." And that was the end of that.

In the mayhem that followed, more than 2,390 American sailors, soldiers, and civilians lost their lives, and almost 1,200 were wounded. Of the 185 ships in Pearl Harbor that morning, 21 were sunk or seriously damaged, including all eight battleships of the Pacific Fleet. The Army and Navy lost 188 aircraft at six airfields. By contrast, about a hundred Japanese airmen and submarine crewmen were killed during the attack, which claimed only 29 Japanese planes, one large submarine, and five midget submarines.

To Yamamoto and the Imperial Navy, Operation Hawaii appeared to be a complete success. Through diligent training, innovative weapon designs, bold strategy, and fearless execution, Japan gained the upper hand during the first months of the war. But it also made some big mistakes. It failed to destroy Pearl Harbor's Navy Yard, which within weeks repaired three battleships and sent them back to sea. It failed to blow up the oil storage tanks, brimming with 190 million gallons. Without that fuel the fleet would have had to relocate to the mainland. Finally, it failed to catch the U.S. Pacific Fleet's three aircraft carriers in port, and within six months the carriers struck back, sinking four Japanese flattops at the Battle of Midway.

Most important for Japan, Yamamoto had misjudged the United States. Instead of being demoralized by the surprise attack, as he had predicted, the American people were enraged. No matter what their political differences, they were now united in their determination to seek revenge. No longer did President Roosevelt have to persuade the U.S. to join the world at war. When the Japanese bombers struck on that awful Sunday morning, they gave Americans all the reason they needed. ★

**Mastermind of Operation Hawaii, Adm. Isoruku Yamamoto begins mapping out plans a year before the attack on Pearl Harbor. His target is the once sleepy naval base transformed by President Franklin D. Roosevelt into a stronghold to deter Japanese aggression in the Pacific. Sailors stationed at Pearl Harbor (opposite) thank their luck for the warm weather and friendly Hawaiian residents. They will soon be targeted by Japanese pilots, one of whom draws a taunting cartoon (above right) depicting the bombing of a U.S. battleship and aircraft carrier.**

ABOARD THE JAPANESE FLEET

For months, squads of Imperial Navy pilots had practiced torpedo runs secretly on the Japanese island of Kyushu. But crews on the carrier task force (below) learn of their actual target only five days away from Oahu. "An air attack on Hawaii! A dream come true!" one seaman says. Many shout *banzais* at the news. Others are frightened but determined. "The moment has arrived," Admiral Yamamoto radios from Japan. "The rise or fall of our empire is at stake." On the flagship *Akagi* an officer unveils a seven-by-seven-foot plaster-of-paris relief map of Pearl Harbor. Pilots test each other with flashcards showing silhouettes of battleships such as the *Oklahoma, West Virginia, California,* and *Arizona.*

At 5:50 a.m. on December 7, Adm. Chuichi Nagumo turns his six carriers into the wind, their decks pitching in the swells. On the *Akagi* Lt. Comdr. Mitsuo Fuchida, leader of the air attack, pulls on a red shirt to conceal potential wounds from his men; he does not want them to be distracted. After a breakfast of *sekihan*, a ceremonial dish of rice with tiny red beans, the pilots tie on *hachimaki* headbands with the words "Certain Victory!" On the carrier *Hiryu* the skipper gives a few last words of encouragement: "This is war between Japan and the United States. Every man must do his duty with a strong heart."

After a 20-minute delay because of the rough weather, the first wave of Zero fighters (right) takes off, blue-white flames shooting from their engine exhaust pipes. Next come the dive-bombers, high-level bombers, and torpedo planes. Within 15 minutes, 183 aircraft are winging toward Oahu, 230 miles to the south. Another 167 planes will follow in the second wave.

## PLAN OF ATTACK

Huddled on the carrier *Kaga,* Japanese pilots (above) study a last-minute sketch of attack routes chalked on the deck. The plan calls for Val dive-bombers and Zero fighters to knock out Oahu's five military airfields, while high-level Kate bombers and torpedo planes pound warships in Pearl Harbor. Pilots from the *Kaga* are assigned to attack the battleships *Tennessee, West Virginia,* and *Arizona,* among other targets. At the same time, two-man Japanese midget submarines are infiltrating the harbor. A Japanese chart (above right) shows harbor depths and a proposed route around Ford Island. On the carrier *Akagi* (right) Comdr. Kanjiro Ono, listening to Hawaiian songs on Honolulu radio station KGMB, hears nothing to suggest that Americans suspect an attack.

## Japanese Air Assault on Oahu

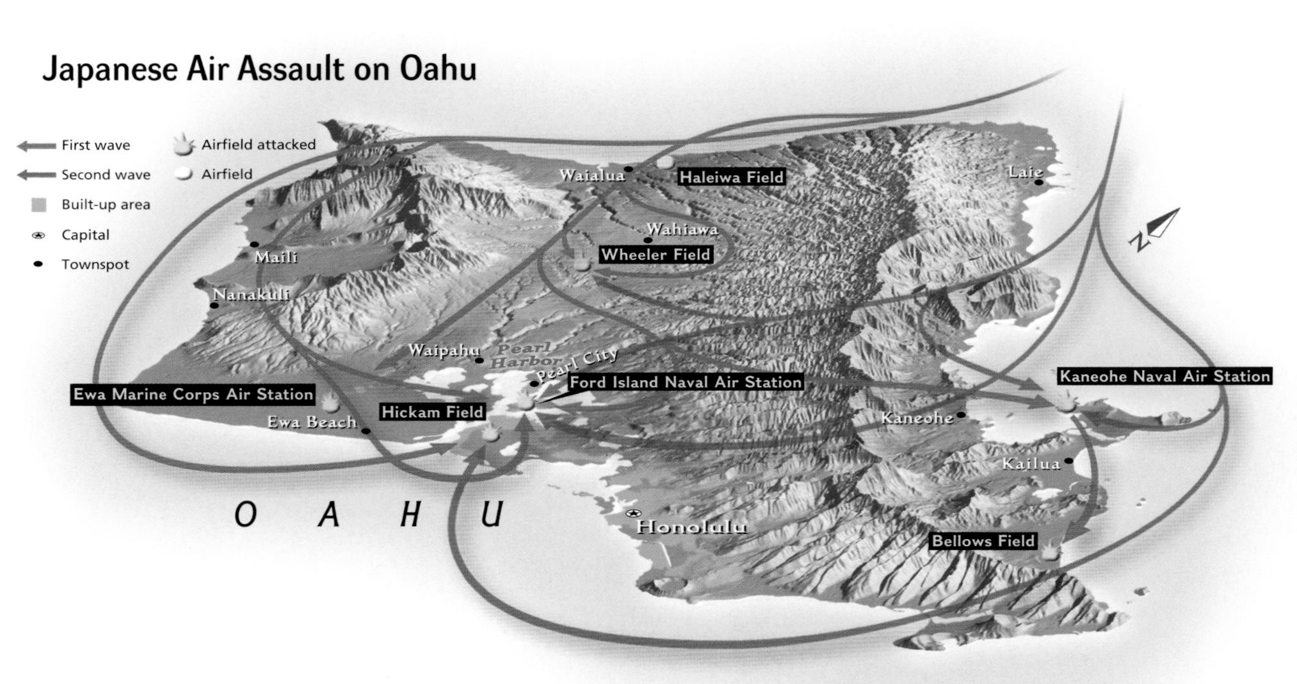


**FIRST WAVE**

As soon as the first wave of Japanese planes reaches Oahu's north coast, flight leader Fuchida, in a Kate bomber with red and yellow stripes on its tail, fires a flare at 7:40 a.m. to start the attack. *"Tora, tora, tora*—Tiger, tiger, tiger," he soon radios to the carrier fleet, signaling they have achieved a complete surprise. Within minutes 25 dive-bombers from the carrier *Zuikaku* hit Wheeler Field (right) with 550-pound bombs, destroying hangars and most of the U.S. Army's fighters. The island's other airfields are also neutralized. Torpedo planes, flying as low as 30 feet, swoop down on Pearl Harbor, dropping Mitsubishi torpedoes specially adapted to run in shallow water. One pilot (far right) pulls up sharply as a plume explodes over the *Oklahoma.* "*Atarimashita!*—It struck!" airmen shout as torpedo after torpedo hits the warships clustered in the harbor.

Hit by three 550-pound bombs, the destroyer *Shaw* erupts in a fireball when her forward magazines ignite. Burning fuel oil spilling from the *West Virginia* (opposite) makes rescue difficult for a launch plucking a sailor from the water. Struck by eight torpedoes, the battleship burns for 24 hours.

THEY WERE IN THIS OIL THAT WAS ON FIRE. THEY WERE TRYING TO SWIM OUT OF IT. THEY'D COME UP AND TRY TO GET THEIR BREATH. . . . THE SKIN ON THEIR FACE WAS JUST FALLING OFF.

—CHARLES CHRISTENSEN/U.S.S. *ARGONNE*

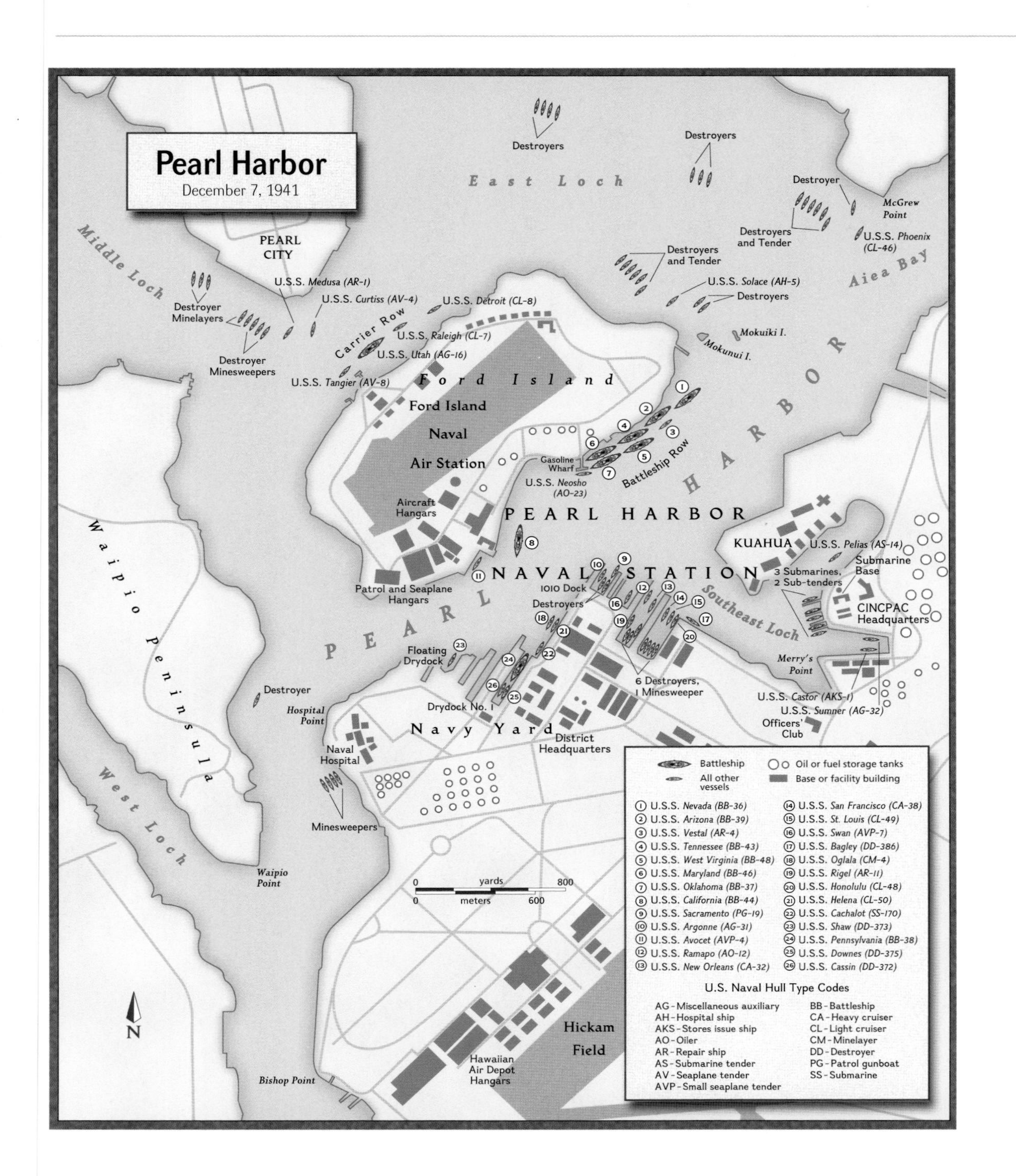




As the musicians of *Nevada*'s 23-man band start to play "The Star-Spangled Banner" at 8 a.m., a torpedo plane strafes them, shredding the flag as it's being raised. They refuse to stop, even as bullets from a second plane splinter the deck at their feet. Looking down from his bomber, Lieutenant Commander Fuchida counts eight battleships in the harbor, but none of the three aircraft carriers he would most like to attack. Smoke from the *Nevada* obscures her deck (opposite, at far right), while oil gushes from the torpedoed *Oklahoma* and *West Virginia*. As the ships begin to roll, crewmen down below in smoke-filled, flooding compartments skid and stumble on the oily, slanting decks. Two splashes near the *Arizona*'s stern show at least one hit by an armor-piercing bomb. Five of the eight battleship captains are still ashore.

By 8:40 the second wave of 167 Japanese warplanes arrives, some dive-bombing the airfields—Ford Island, Kaneohe, Hickam, Ewa, Bellows, and Wheeler—others attacking ships in the harbor. Taking off from a small airstrip at Haleiwa, 2nd Lts. Ken Taylor and George Welch fought back in their P-40 fighters, downing six Japanese planes. Three city firemen are killed at Hickam when they respond to what they believed was a three-alarm blaze. On Ford Island the fire brigade discovers it has no water pressure to fight hangar blazes because the *Arizona* has sunk on the island's water mains, crushing them.

Smoke from the Navy Yard and Ford Island obscures targets for the second wave of Japanese bombers, which is met by a wall of antiaircraft fire when it arrives an hour after the first wave. Sailors on the ships and docks (opposite) also took up small arms to fight back.

WE CLIMBED AS FAST AS WE COULD, FOR THE STEEL OF THE MAST WAS HOT FROM NEARBY FIRES. . . .

I ATTACHED THE NATION'S COLORS AND HOISTED THEM. . . . WE TURNED . . . AND SAW

ANOTHER WAVE OF JAPANESE PLANES STRAFING HIS WAY TO OUR POSITION.

—M. JOSEPH MCDONALD/U.S.S. *TENNESSEE*

CLARKE SIMMONS

I SAW A PLANE MAKING A RUN ON THE *UTAH.* AS HE DROPPED HIS TORPEDO, THE WING DIPPED, AND HE STRAIGHTENED UP. THE TORPEDO HIT. AND THEN CAME ANOTHER PLANE AND DROPPED ANOTHER TORPEDO. THINGS WERE BREAKING LOOSE. FURNITURE WAS SLIDING AROUND. WE HEARD THE BUGLER BLOW THE CALL FOR "ABANDON SHIP." WE BEGAN TO SWIM TOWARD FORD ISLAND. THEY WERE MACHINE-GUNNING US FROM TWO DIRECTIONS. I SAW FELLOWS YELLING AND SCREAMING. —CLARKE SIMMONS, U.S.S. *UTAH*

As fireboats battle flames on Battleship Row (left), a dozen unarmed U.S. B-17 bombers fly in from the mainland. Dodging Japanese fighters and friendly fire, this one lands safely at Hickam Field. A car racing to Kaneohe Naval Air Station (above right) finds seaplanes set afire by Japanese Zeroes.

I WAS IN MY CABIN COMMENCING TO DRESS, WHEN . . . THE MARINE ORDERLY RUSHED INTO THE CABIN AND ANNOUNCED, "THE JAPANESE ARE ATTACKING US." THERE WAS ANOTHER HEAVY EXPLOSION THAT THREW ME FLAT ON THE DECK. . . . [I] HAD JUST GOTTEN TO MY FEET AGAIN WHEN THERE WAS A TERRIFIC FLASH OF FLAME FROM THE *ARIZONA.* —COMDR. R. H. HILLENKOETTER, U.S.S. *WEST VIRGINIA*

THE SHIP WAS ALREADY ROLLING OVER ON US. WE JUMPED INTO THE WATER. IT WAS ONLY ABOUT A FIVE-FOOT JUMP. I SAW THE SHIP AND THE BIG GUN TURRETS COMING DOWN ON ME, AND I BEGAN TO SWIM AS FAST AS I COULD. THE SHIP ROLLED OVER. THERE IT WAS, KEEL UP. I WAS SURE THAT MANY OF MY SHIPMATES WERE TRAPPED INSIDE. —GEORGE SMITH, U.S.S. *OKLAHOMA*

**GEORGE SMITH**

ABOUT MONDAY NOON WE HEARD TAPPING, AND WE ANSWERED THEM. AFTER SO LONG THEY WERE RIGHT OVERHEAD, AND WE COULD HEAR THEM TALKING. WHEN THEY STARTED TO CUT INTO US, IT LET OUT OUR AIR . . . THE WATER CAME UP AS OUR AIR ESCAPED. . . . BUT WE STILL HAVE ABOUT SIX INCHES OF AIR SPACE. WE TRIED THE LINEN ROOM AGAIN AND IT GAVE A LITTLE. . . . WE WENT IN AND STARTED TAPPING AGAIN. THE RESCUERS SOON GOT TO US. —W. F. STAFF, U.S.S. *OKLAHOMA*

A day after the attack workmen on the capsized battleship *Oklahoma* (right) rescue 32 sailors trapped inside. The destroyers *Cassin* and *Downes* lie in a tangle (left) in dry dock after a fuel-oil fire set off their depth charges. Fireboats fight lingering blazes for days.

CLAIRE BECKER

WE WERE PLANNING TO GO ON A PICNIC. I HAD MARRIED PAUL BECKER, A BRAND-NEW MARINE FIRST LIEUTENANT IN OCTOBER. . . . THE SOUND OF GUNFIRE AWAKENED ME. I LOOKED OUT THE WINDOW AND SAW THAT THE SKY WAS FULL OF GRAY SMOKE. THEN A SMALL PLANE—A JAPANESE TORPEDO PLANE—WENT RIGHT BY THE WINDOW. YOU COULD SEE THE PILOT, GRINNING A LITTLE. —CLAIRE BECKER

Honolulu Star-Bulletin 1st EXTRA

# WAR!

SAN FRANCISCO, Dec. 7.—President Roosevelt announced this morning that Japanese planes had attacked Manila and Pearl Harbor.

# OAHU BOMBED BY JAPANESE PLANES

SIX KNOWN DEAD, 21 INJURED, AT EMERGENCY HOSPITAL

Attack Made On Island's Defense Areas

Hundreds See City Bombed

Names of Dead and Injured

Schools Closed

Editorial

WHEN WE RECOGNIZED THE RISING-SUN INSIGNIA AND HEARD THE EXPLOSIONS START TO GO OFF, WE PUSHED THE BEDS BACK INTO THE WARD. . . . A LINE OF BULLETS WAS CUTTING A PATH FROM THE GROUND AND UP THE SIDE OF THE BUILDING. TWO HEAVY BULLETS LODGED IN THE DOOR FRAME, RIGHT WHERE MY KNEES WOULD HAVE BEEN. JUST A FRACTION OF A SECOND LONGER, AND THE STRAFING WOULD HAVE CUT ME OFF AT THE KNEES. I ALMOST BECAME A PATIENT IN MY OWN WARD. —MYRTLE WATSON, SCHOFIELD BARRACKS HOSPITAL

Five miles from Pearl Harbor three civilians die when their Packard is riddled by shrapnel from a U.S. Navy antiaircraft shell. More shells fall on Honolulu, killing an additional 35 residents. Overwhelmed by wounded servicemen, medics borrow pickup trucks for ambulances and turn schools into emergency wards.

ARIZ
2
2
ML

# The *Arizona:* End of an Era

Battleships ruled the seas when the *Arizona* was commissioned in 1916. Her twelve 14-inch guns, deployed in four turrets, could each blast a 1,400-pound shell 20 miles. With some 12,500 tons of armored plate to protect her and a crew of more than 1,500 to serve her, she could cruise 15,650 miles without refueling. Steaming at the head of a battle line (right) with the *Nevada, Tennessee, New Mexico, Mississippi,* and *Idaho* in the 1930s, she projected the power of the United States wherever she sailed. For that reason, in 1940 President Roosevelt positioned her, along with the rest of the Pacific Fleet, in Hawaii to discourage Japanese moves against European colonies in Southeast Asia. And for the same reason, Admiral Yamamoto targeted her and the other battleships at Pearl Harbor as symbols of American strength. Yet even as *Arizona* moored at Quay F-7 beside Ford Island on Friday, December 5, the era she represented—when great battlewagons ruled the seas—was about to end. The age of aircraft carriers was about to arrive—in two days' time—on the wings of carrier-borne planes delivering devastation from the skies.

Despite her thick armor, the *Arizona* suffers a fatal blow when a 1,760-pound armor-piercing shell stabs through her forward decks, detonating just above the powder magazines for the ship's big guns. In the blast that follows, 500 tons of explosives gut the battleship, sending a massive fireball into the sky and raining debris and body parts down on nearby ships. Most of the 1,177 men who die on the *Arizona* perish in that instant. All but 229, whose bodies are recovered in the days after the attack, remain entombed in the ship. A clock salvaged from the wreckage still reads 8:05.

Decades later, when divers from the National Park Service examine the site, they find live shells in the mud, as well as the 14-inch guns from a forward turret (right). At least a half million gallons of No. 6 fuel oil also remains trapped in a band of fuel bunkers lining the 608-foot-long ship's outer hull. Designed to help protect the *Arizona* from torpedoes, these corroding bunkers now pose a potential environmental risk. The Park Service, which manages the site, estimates that a quart of oil a day leaks into the harbor. Officials continue to monitor the wreck for signs of further deterioration.

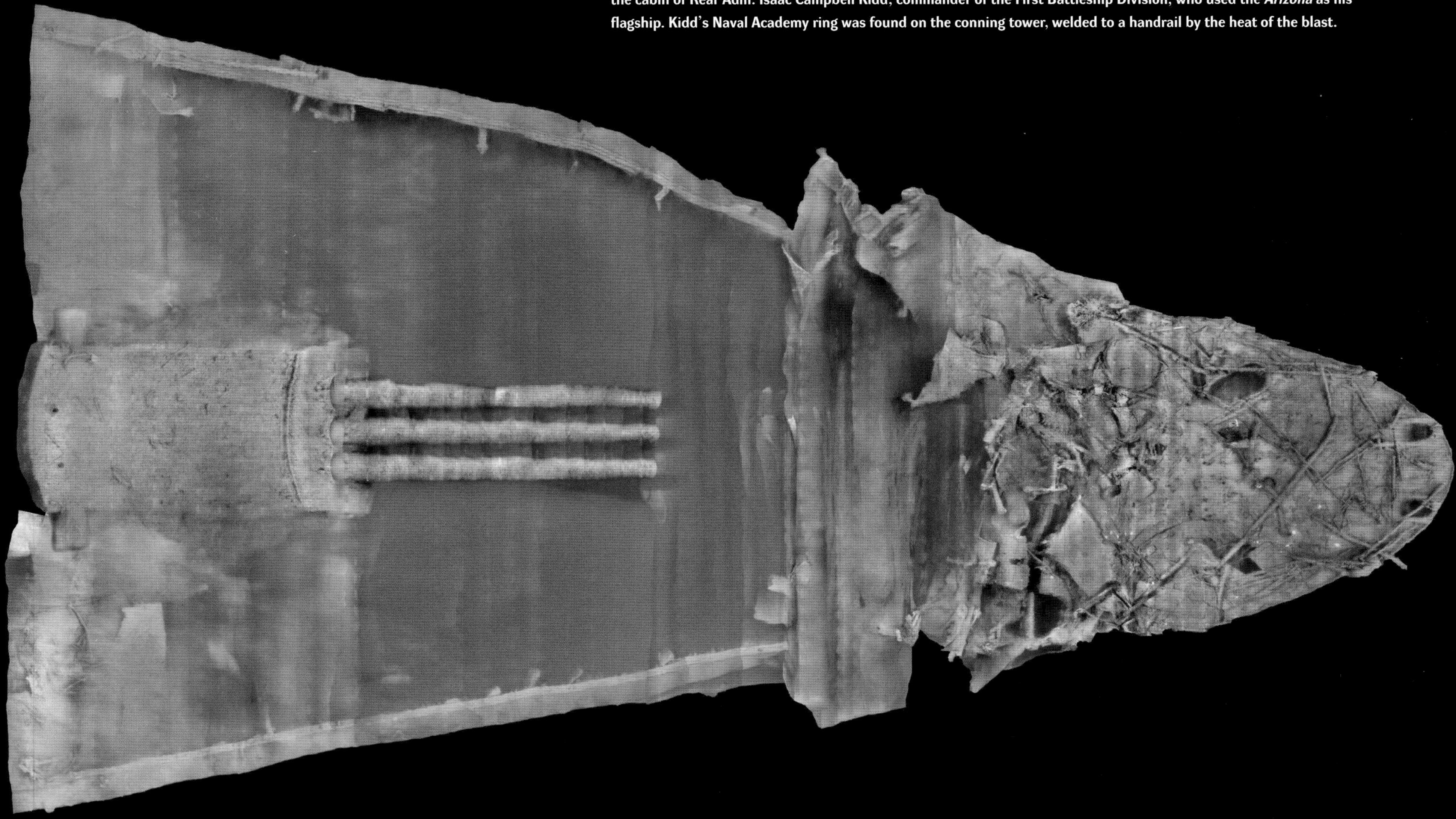

The crumpled bow of the *Arizona* testifies to the power of the explosion that shredded the deck and hull of the battleship. Created from dozens of digital video images compiled by computer, this underwater mosaic shows the guns of turret I resting on the collapsed deck below. Because of the murkiness of the harbor, such a view would be impossible with conventional photographs. In another project a team of photoengineers from National Geographic, collaborating with the National Park Service, used television cameras to inspect the ship's interior spaces, including the cabin of Rear Adm. Isaac Campbell Kidd, commander of the First Battleship Division, who used the *Arizona* as his flagship. Kidd's Naval Academy ring was found on the conning tower, welded to a handrail by the heat of the blast.

Like a bridge spanning the years, the *Arizona* Memorial (opposite), has become a place of reconciliation as well as remembrance. About 1.5 million visitors, including some 300,000 Japanese tourists, come here each year to pay their respects. A volunteer at the memorial, Dick Fiske (above, at right) was a Marine bugler preparing to sound colors from the bridge of the nearby *West Virginia* when the attack began. His ship was struck by eight torpedoes and two bombs. One bomb plunged through a gun turret and came to rest, unexploded, on top of the ship's ammunition storage. "We were very fortunate," Fiske says. Zenji Abe, at left, first saw the U.S. battleships from the cockpit of his dive-bomber. After meeting at a reunion in 1991, the two men became friends. Every month for the past decade, Abe has had two roses placed in front of the memorial's roster of those who died (left), and Fiske plays taps over the flowers.

Remembering the perils of war has a profound effect upon all who visit the site, says Daniel Martinez, the National Park Service's historian at the memorial. During a recent ceremony with officials from Japan, he recalls, "I was standing amidst 150 or more Japanese officers and thought to myself how strange it was to be standing here, and yet how meaningful and how hopeful, how far we have come."

# Search for a Midget Sub

Before he leaves Kure, Japan, Ensign Kazuo Sakamaki buys a small bottle of perfume for his dangerous mission. He intends to splash some on before going into battle, so he can die gloriously "like cherry blossoms falling to the ground." He and nine others are assigned to five midget submarines, each armed with two torpedoes, to infiltrate Pearl Harbor before the attack. "We had fully expected to die in battle," Sakamaki (above) later writes. "Then something went wrong."

The gyrocompass on Sakamaki's two-man sub malfunctions, sending Chief Warrant Officer Kiyoshi Inagaki and him on a 30-hour wild-goose chase that ends when their battery-driven vessel runs aground at Waimanalo, Oahu, near Bellows Field. Inagaki drowns, but Sakamaki survives to become the United States' first prisoner of World War II.

None of the other midget subs return either. One is later salvaged in Keehi Lagoon (left) by the U.S.S. *Current.* Another was attacked and presumably sunk by the U.S.S. *Ward* more than an hour before the Japanese air raid. In November 2000 the National Geographic Society sponsors underwater explorer Robert D. Ballard to search for the wrecked sub in 1,200 feet of water. With the Honolulu skyline behind him, Mark DeRoche (right), a deck engineer, prepares *Argus*, a deep-water imaging vehicle, for the job. Although the expedition locates a seaplane, a fighter, and a tank on the bottom, it discovers no signs of the midget sub.

## National Geographic magazine

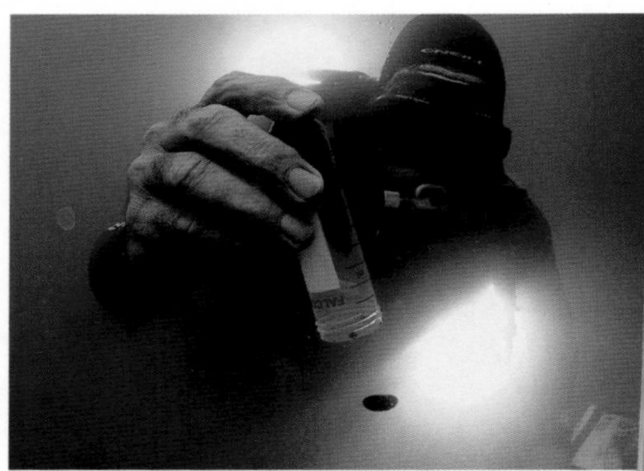

Do globules of oil leaking from the wreck of the *Arizona* pose an environmental problem in Pearl Harbor? Senior Writer Priit Vesilind reports in the June 2001 NATIONAL GEOGRAPHIC.

## National Geographic Television

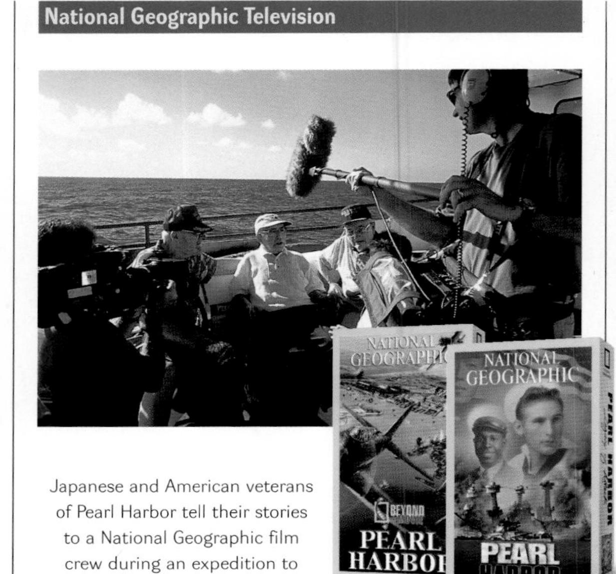


Japanese and American veterans of Pearl Harbor tell their stories to a National Geographic film crew during an expedition to find a Japanese midget submarine lost in the attack.

## National Geographic Books

Explorer Robert D. Ballard searches for the wrecks of World War II naval battles; Thomas B. Allen retells tales of Pearl Harbor for children.

## National Geographic Maps

The "Pearl Harbor Sixtieth Anniversary Commemorative Map" puts the attack in perspective with a fact-filled poster on one side and a 1942 war map on the other.

## nationalgeographic.com

In addition to the Society's films, books, and magazine, *nationalgeographic.com* presents a full menu of interactive Pearl Harbor features.

TO ORDER A NATIONAL GEOGRAPHIC BOOK, VIDEO, OR MAP, CALL

**1-888-CALL-NGS** (1-888-225-5647)

PLEASE USE SOURCE CODE: **PH0701**